Linda Ronstadt's Exceptional Career

By

Dayle Peters

Copyright © 2023

Table of Content

Chapter 1: 2
   Early Life 3
Chapter 2: 12
Chapter 3: 21
   Beginning of professional career 21
Chapter 4: 26
Chapter 5 35
   Touring 35
Chapter 6: 38
   Relationships 38
Chapter 7: 56
   Political Views 56
Chapter 8: 63
   Achievements 63
Chapter 9: 78
   Conclusion 78

Chapter 1:

Early Life

Linda Ronstadt was born on July 15, 1946, in Tucson, Arizona. raised on the family's 10-acre ranch with her siblings Peter, Michael, and Gretchen. From an early age, she was exposed to Mexican-American culture, which heavily influenced her music. At the age of 11, Linda began singing with her siblings in a folk trio, performing in local shows and festivals. She was particularly influenced by traditional Mexican music, as well as country, rock, and folk.

Linda Ronstadt attended the University of Arizona, Tucson, from 1967-1971. During her time at the University, Linda studied Latin American history and Spanish, as well as music. Her time at the University was an important part of her musical journey and her successful career.

At the University of Arizona, Linda met many people who became important to her life and career. She met and befriended, guitarist Kenny Edwards and they formed a folk trio with another student, Bob Kimmel. The trio performed at local coffeehouses and bars, gaining local popularity and recognition.

Linda also had the opportunity to study music theory and vocal lessons while at the University of Arizona. She studied classical music theory, voice, and opera techniques to become a professional singer. She was also exposed to more traditional Mexican music, which would later become an important part of her musical repertoire.

Linda also used her time at the University of Arizona to explore her musical interests. She was exposed to different musical styles and genres and was able to experiment with her own music. She also doped her songwriting skills and was able to craft her songs.

The University of Arizona also provided Linda with exposure to the Tucson music scene. She was able to attend many concerts, as well as to perform in some of the local bars and venues. She also made connections with local musicians and was able to collaborate with them on her music.

Linda Ronstadt's time at the University of Arizona was invaluable to her music career. It was a great opportunity for her to gain knowledge, experience, and contacts that she would need for her future success. Her time at the University of Arizona was an important part of her journey to becoming a successful singer and songwriter.

Linda Ronstadt's father, Gilbert Ronstadt, came from a pioneering Arizona ranching family. His ancestors were of Mexican descent and had a German male ancestor. Gilbert Ronstadt was the son of a Mexican father and a German mother, who were both born in Arizona. He was raised in a large family with siblings and cousins and was an integral part of the pioneering spirit of the Ronstadt family.

Gilbert Ronstadt was a hardworking rancher, who managed the family's cattle, sheep, and horses. He was an expert in equine care, and he taught Linda the basics of horsemanship. He also passed down his knowledge of Mexican culture, including music, to his daughter. Gilbert was a devout Catholic and was an active member of the local church.

An avid music lover, Gilbert Ronstadt was an early influence on Linda's musical career. He listened to traditional Mexican music and would often take Linda to music and dance performances. He also exposed her to a variety of musical genres, including country, jazz, and classical. Gilbert's love of music inspired Linda to pursue a musical career and eventually become one of the most successful female singers of the 1970s.

Linda Ronstadt was deeply influenced by the pioneering spirit of her father. He instilled in her a strong work ethic and taught her the importance of being independent and self-reliant. He also gave her a deep appreciation for the culture and music of her Mexican heritage. His influence and guidance helped shape Linda into the successful artist she is today.

Linda Ronstadt's father was a vital part of her life and career. He was a dedicated rancher, a passionate music lover, and a devoted Catholic. He instilled in Linda his pioneering spirit and helped her to develop her unique style. Gilbert Ronstadt was an integral part of Linda's success, and his memory will always be cherished.

Linda Ronstadt's mother Ruth Mary was of German, English, and Dutch ancestry. Her family was raised in Flint, Michigan, an industrial city located in the southeastern corner of the state. Ruth Mary was an incredibly strong woman, who worked hard to provide for her family during the difficult times of the Great Depression. She was a homemaker but also worked at a variety of other jobs to help make ends meet. She was known for her generosity and her kind spirit and was highly respected in the community.

Ruth Mary was a great role model for her daughter Linda. She taught her the importance of hard work, patience, and perseverance. Ruth Mary also taught Linda to be kind to others and to always strive for success. She was also a great listener, always encouraging Linda to follow her dreams and pursue her passion for music. Ruth Mary was a great supporter of Linda's music career, often attending her concerts and cheering her on.

Ruth Mary was also passionate about the environment and was an avid supporter of conservation. She loved to spend time outside, enjoying nature and discovering the beauty in the world around her. She was a great example to Linda, teaching her to appreciate and respect the environment.

Ruth Mary was a beloved member of the community and was highly respected for her dedication and hard work. She was a strong and independent woman, who worked hard to provide for her family. She was brave in the face of adversity, and her example of strength and perseverance was a great inspiration to her daughter Linda.

Ruth Mary was a loving and caring mother to Linda. She was always there for Linda, providing support and guidance. Her encouragement and positive attitude enabled Linda to pursue her dreams and achieve her goals. She was a great example of a strong and independent woman, who worked hard and was always willing to lend a helping hand to those in need. Ruth Mary was the proud mother of Linda Ronstadt and was an inspiration to many.

Linda Ronstadt's great-grandfather, Friedrich August Ronstadt, was an engineer who immigrated to Tucson, Arizona in 1856. He was born in 1834 in Dortmund, Germany, and had a great interest in engineering and mechanics. He was a self-taught engineer who worked as a farmer and miner before starting his own business in Tucson. Friedrich was responsible for the construction of several Tucson landmarks, including the city's first waterworks, the Ronstadt Building, and the first Pima County Courthouse. He was also part of the team that built the Southern Pacific Railroad from Tucson to Phoenix.

Friedrich Ronstadt was an innovator and an early entrepreneur in Tucson. He was one of the first people to bring modern technology to the area and he was instrumental in the development of Tucson's infrastructure. Despite having no formal training, he was able to build and maintain complex machines that were essential to the city's growth. He was also a philanthropist and was known for his generosity to the people of Tucson.

Throughout his life, Friedrich Ronstadt was a leader in the Tucson community. He was a founding member of the Tucson Chamber of Commerce and a major contributor to the city's economy. He was also a leader in the German-American community and was respected by members of all backgrounds. Friedrich was a devout Catholic and was active in the local church.

Friedrich Ronstadt was a successful businessman, a respected community leader, and a beloved family man. He was a major contributor to the development of Tucson and he helped shape the city's culture and identity. He passed away in

1912, leaving behind a legacy of innovation and community service. His great-granddaughter, Linda Ronstadt, has continued the family tradition of excellence and leadership.

Peter is the eldest of the four Ronstadt siblings, followed by Linda, Michael, and Suzy. Growing up, Peter was a star athlete at Tucson High School, playing football and basketball. He then attended the University of Arizona, where he earned a degree in criminal justice.

After college, Peter began his career with the Tucson Police Department in 1970. His rise through the ranks was rapid, and in 1981 he was appointed Chief of Police. He served in this position until 1991 when he left to pursue other interests. During his tenure, Peter worked hard to improve the Tucson Police Department and make it a more efficient and effective organization.

Throughout his time as Chief of Police, Peter was a strong advocate for community policing and neighborhood policing. He was also very vocal in his support for the use of technology to better serve the Tucson community. He helped modernize the police department, providing officers with access to the latest weapons, vehicles, and equipment.

Chapter 2:

Early Career Influences

Linda Ronstadt's early family life was filled with music and tradition. She was born in Tucson, Arizona, in 1946, to Gilbert and Ruth Mary Ronstadt, both of whom were of Mexican heritage. Her father was a renowned musician, and he taught Linda to play the guitar and harmonica, as well as to sing. He also passed on his love of traditional Mexican folk music to his daughter.

Linda was surrounded by music from a young age. Her father was a popular figure in the local music scene, playing on the local radio and in small clubs across Tucson. He was also an accomplished mariachi musician, and Linda learned to play mariachi music as a child. Music was a central part of the family's life, and Linda was exposed to traditional Mexican and

American music, as well as jazz and classical music.

Linda's mother was an accomplished dancer, and she encouraged Linda to take dance lessons as a child. She also taught Linda to appreciate traditional Mexican dances, such as the jarabe tapatio, which Linda would later perform in her concerts.

Linda's family was deeply religious. Her parents were devout Catholics, and the family attended mass every Sunday. Linda learned the importance of faith and prayer from her parents, and she would later incorporate these beliefs into her music.

Linda's early family life was also filled with tradition. Her parents celebrated Mexican holidays, such as Cinco de Mayo and Dia de los Muertos, and Linda learned to appreciate the customs and traditions of her heritage. Her father also taught her the traditional songs of his homeland, and Linda became proficient in singing traditional Mexican songs.

Linda's early family life was filled with music, faith, and tradition. This foundation laid the groundwork for Linda's later success as a singer and songwriter. She was surrounded by music from a young age, and she was encouraged to express her creativity and explore different styles of music. Her family instilled the importance of faith and tradition, which helped shape her musical identity. Linda Ronstadt's early family life was an important part of her musical journey.

Ronstadt has remarked that everything she has recorded on her records – rock and roll, rhythm and blues, gospel, opera, country, choral, and mariachi – is all music she heard her family sing in their living room or heard played on the radio. This eclectic mix of styles has made Ronstadt one of the most beloved singers of the last fifty years. She has explored a variety of genres, from folk-rock to country-rock to jazz and even mariachi. Her voice has been described as a "bel canto instrument" that can convey the emotion of the song with effortless clarity.

Ronstadt's vocal range is vast, encompassing three octaves and five notes. She has a special gift for capturing the spirit and emotion of a song and conveying it to the listener. Her vocal style is powerful and passionate, yet nuanced and sensitive. She has been known to use a variety of vocal techniques to get the desired effect, such as vibrato and controlled vibrato, falsetto, and vibrato-like effects.

She credits her mother for her love of Gilbert and Sullivan, a light opera duo, and her father for introducing her to the classic pop and Great American Songbook repertoire. As a young girl, Linda was exposed to the music of Gilbert and Sullivan as well as other musical theater composers, which would have a profound effect on her musical identity.

Linda's mother, Gilberta, was a passionate fan of Gilbert and Sullivan's operettas. She would often sing the pieces with her daughter, exposing Linda to the intricate harmonies and witty lyrics of the duo. Linda was enamored with the music, and it likely had a profound influence on her musical tastes and style.

Linda's father, Gilbert, was also influential in the formation of her musical identity. He had a deep appreciation for classic pop and the Great American Songbook, and he would often take Linda to see live performances of these artists. These experiences helped to spark Linda's interest in these musical genres, and as she got older, she began to incorporate them into her singing style.

At the age of 18, Linda moved to Los Angeles, where she began to pursue a career in music. She was quickly noticed by several producers and record labels, who saw potential in her unique voice and style. Her first album was released in 1969, and it featured a mix of folk and rock music. However, it was her follow-up album, Heart Like a Wheel, that truly established Linda as a star. The album featured a mix of country rock, folk, and the Great American

Songbook standards that Linda had been exposed to as a child.

The success of Heart Like a Wheel made Linda a household name, and she quickly became one of the most successful singers of the 1970s. She began to incorporate more traditional pop and Great American Songbook standards into her music, and her albums featured covers of songs by artists such as Cole Porter, Irving Berlin, and George Gershwin. This helped to revive interest in the Great American Songbook and traditional pop music, and Linda soon became a symbol of this resurgence.

Linda Ronstadt's success and influence can be attributed to her parents, who introduced her to the music that would come to define her career. Her mother's passion for Gilbert and Sullivan and her father's appreciation for classic pop and the Great American Songbook were instrumental in the formation of Linda's own musical identity. Thanks to their influence, Linda was able to help revive the Great American Songbook and traditional pop music, and reintroduce them to an entire generation.

Her unique style of singing has been heavily influenced by other great vocalists such as Lola Beltrán and Édith Piaf. Both of these singers had a profound impact on Ronstadt's style, and she has often cited their singing and rhythms as being "more like Greek music or opera music".

Beltrán, who was born in Mexico in 1932, was renowned for her powerful and emotive singing style. Her influence on Ronstadt is evident in her rendition of the traditional Mexican song 'Cielito Lindo', where she captures the essence of Beltrán's style while adding her unique spin to the classic tune. This is just one of many examples of Ronstadt's incorporation of Beltrán's style into her own.

Similarly, the French vocalist Édith Piaf had a major influence on Ronstadt's singing. She has cited Piaf's passionate and emotive delivery as one of her major inspirations. Ronstadt has also been greatly inspired by Piaf's signature song 'La Vie en Rose', covering the song multiple times over the course of her career. Ronstadt's recording of the song is a testament to her ability to capture the raw emotion of Piaf's original while adding her unique style to the classic.

Ronstadt has also taken influence from many other singers, including Mexican ranchera singers, American folk singers, and even the Beatles. Her ability to incorporate so many different styles into her singing has made her one of the most unique and influential vocalists of her generation. Her unique singing style, which has been heavily influenced by Lola Beltrán and Édith Piaf, has helped her to become a legendary vocalist and one of the most beloved singers of all time.

Ronstadt drew influence from country singer Hank Williams, whose songs she often covered. She was drawn to his lyrical style and his ability to convey emotion through his music. Ronstadt's renditions of Williams' songs, such as "I Can't Help It (If I'm Still in Love With You)" and "Your Cheatin' Heart," became major hits. She also frequently included his songs in her live performances.

Throughout her career, Ronstadt was known for her willingness to take risks and defy musical conventions. She often experimented with different musical styles, incorporating elements of rock, pop, R&B, and Latin music into her songs. She also collaborated with numerous artists, including Dolly Parton, Emmylou Harris, Neil Young, and Johnny Cash. In the late 1970s and early 1980s, Ronstadt ventured into disco and even opera.

In addition to her musical versatility, Ronstadt was also known for her political activism. In the early 1970s, she joined the boycott of Arizona over its refusal to recognize Martin Luther King Jr. Day. In the 1980s, she was an outspoken advocate for women's rights and gay rights.

Linda Ronstadt's influence on American music is undeniable. She made a name for herself as a pioneering female artist and a risk-taker who defied expectations. With her powerful voice and her eclectic range of styles, she was able to bridge the gap between country, folk, rock, and pop music. Her influence can be heard in the music of countless artists today, including Taylor Swift and Adele. Ronstadt's music and her activism will continue to inspire generations to come.

Chapter 3:

Beginning of professional career

Linda Ronstadt is a legendary singer, songwriter, and producer who has had a long and successful career spanning decades. Born in 1946 in Tucson, Arizona, she was the daughter of a Mexican father and a German mother. She began her musical career at an early age, forming a folk trio with her brother Peter and sister Gretchen when she was just 14.

Linda Ronstadt and her group were a unique and iconic presence in the music scene of the late 1960s and early 1970s. The group was comprised of Linda Ronstadt (vocals and guitar), Kenny Edwards (guitar, mandolin, and vocals), Gilbert Ronstadt (Linda's brother; guitar and vocals), and Bobby Kimmel (bass and vocals).

The group's sound was heavily influenced by country rock, folk, and bluegrass, and featured Linda's soulful and unique vocal style. Linda Ronstadt and her group played coffeehouses, fraternity houses, and other small venues, billing themselves as "the Union City Ramblers" and "The Three Ronstadts", and they even recorded themselves at a Tucson studio under the name "the New Union Ramblers".

The group's performances featured a mix of covers and original tunes, and their songs often featured complex vocal harmonies, intricate instrumental passages, and tight arrangements. They often included traditional folk ballads, classic country songs, and some of Linda's original compositions.

Linda Ronstadt and her group gained a steady following and were known for their high-energy performances. The group was also known to be very tight-knit; they had an easygoing dynamic that allowed them to work together with ease.

Though the group played mostly in small venues, they did have some success with their recordings. Their first album, "Silk Purse", was released in 1970 and was well-received by critics. The album featured a mix of classic country covers and some of Linda's original tunes.

The group's second album, "Linda Ronstadt and the Stone Poneys", was released in 1971 and featured the hit single "Different Drum". This song helped to bring Linda and her group a wider audience and increased their popularity.

Though Linda Ronstadt and her group disbanded in 1971, their influence on the music scene was long-lasting. They helped to create a unique sound that was heavily influenced by country rock, folk, and bluegrass. Linda's distinctive vocal style and the group's tight arrangements and intricate vocal harmonies set them apart from other bands of the time.

Bobby Kimmel had already established a career in music by the time he was signed to Capitol Records. He was born in New York City in 1945 and grew up in Long Island where he began playing music at an early age. As a teenager, he started to play the electric guitar and perform in local clubs. After high school, he formed a folk-rock band called The New Society. Throughout the early 1960s, he toured and recorded with various bands, and in 1965, he co-founded the folk-rock trio, The Stone Poneys, with Linda Ronstadt and Kenny Edwards.

The trio released their debut album, The Stone Poneys, in 1967, which featured several of Bobby Kimmel's compositions. The album was a critical and commercial success, and the single "Different Drum," written by Kimmel and Edwards, reached the Top Twenty. The trio recorded two more albums, Linda Ronstadt, Stone Poneys and Friends (1968) and Evergreen, Volume 2 (1969).

The group is best remembered for its hit single "Different Drum" (written by Michael Nesmith before he joined the Monkees), which reached number 13 on the Billboard Hot 100 chart as well as number 12 in Cashbox magazine.

The Stone Ponies released their self-titled debut album in 1968, which was followed by a second album, "The Stone Ponies Again", in 1969. The band also released two additional singles, "Send in the Clowns" and "Ride a White Swan". Despite the success of "Different Drum", neither single charted.

Chapter 4:

Solo Career

The Stone Poneys band's disbandment in 1968, Ronstadt embarked on a solo career and released her first solo album, Hand Sown... Home Grown, in 1969.

Hand Sown... Home Grown is an album that showcases Ronstadt's unique vocal range and skill as a musician. The album consists of ten original compositions, as well as covers of classic songs such as "Long Long Time" and "Will You Love Me Tomorrow." Ronstadt's songwriting is unique in that she blends traditional folk, country, and rock genres, creating a sound that is both familiar and new. This album was a major success and is considered to be one of the first albums to bridge the gap between country and rock music.

The album features Ronstadt's signature vocals, as well as some stellar guitar and string accompaniment. Tracks such as "The Only Mama That'll Walk the Line" and "Long Long Time" showcase Ronstadt's songwriting, with their soulful and heartfelt lyrics. Other songs, such as "Silver Threads and Golden Needles" and "Will You Love Me Tomorrow" show off her impressive vocal range and ability to interpret classic songs.

The production of the album was handled by Kenny Edwards, who was also a member of The Stone Poneys. Edwards helped to bring out the best in Ronstadt's voice, as well as her songwriting. His production style was very organic, giving the album a warm and intimate sound.

Hand Sown... Home Grown was a major success and is considered to be the beginning of Ronstadt's successful career.

The album was a critical and commercial success and is highly regarded as one of the best albums of 1969. It was certified Gold by the RIAA and is a testament to Ronstadt's skill as a musician and songwriter.

Linda Ronstadt's Hand Sown... Home Grown is an album that deserves to be remembered as a classic. It is an album that pushed the boundaries of country and rock music and helped to bridge the gap between the two genres. It is a testament to Ronstadt's skill and songwriting and is a must-listen for any music fan.

Linda Ronstadt's Hand Sown ... Home Grown is an iconic record that has been referred to as the first alternative country record by a female recording artist. The album was recorded with a group of musicians that included guitarists Glenn Frey and Bernie Leadon, both of whom would soon join the Eagles. The album was produced by John Boylan, who had previously produced Ronstadt's band, The Stone Poneys, and was recorded in Los Angeles, California.

The album featured a mix of country, folk, and rock influences, with Ronstadt's distinctive voice a notable highlight. The album included covers of songs by Bob Dylan, Johnny Cash, and Jimmie Rodgers, as well as originals penned by Ronstadt and her collaborators.

The album was a commercial success and was certified gold within two months of its release. It also earned Ronstadt her first Grammy nomination for Best Female Country Vocal Performance. In addition to its commercial success, Hand Sown ... Home Grown has been critically acclaimed as well. It has been called a groundbreaking record for its mix of country and folk influences and has been credited with helping to shape the sound of the alternative country in the years to come.

The album is often cited as one of Ronstadt's best and has been included on several lists of essential albums, including Rolling Stone's 500 Greatest Albums of All Time. It has also been included in the National Recording Registry of the Library of Congress, which recognizes recordings that are "culturally, historically, or aesthetically significant."

In the 1970s, Ronstadt was part of the "super session" project known as Free Creek. Free Creek was a series of live jam sessions held in a sound studio in Los Angeles, organized by producer and engineer David Rubinson. It was a unique experiment in which a wide variety of well-known and emerging musicians convened to play and record music, often with little or no rehearsal.

Ronstadt's involvement in Free Creek was a pivotal moment in her career. It was the first time she was able to showcase her vocal talents and demonstrate her innovative approach to music. She took part in several tracks, including a remake of Johnny Cash's "Ring of Fire" and a cover of the Rolling Stones' "Wild Horses." Her contributions to the project provided a glimpse of the musical direction she would follow in the coming years.

In addition to her work on Free Creek, Ronstadt also contributed vocals to some commercials during this period. She most notably sang in a Remington electric razor commercial, in which she and Frank Zappa sing about the razor "cleaning you, thrilling you, and even keeping you from getting busted." Ronstadt's vocals in the commercial showcased her powerful and versatile voice, and it brought her increased attention in the music industry.

Ronstadt's involvement in Free Creek was a crucial step in her career. Not only did it provide a platform for her to showcase her unique approach to music, but it also helped her gain wider recognition in the music industry. Her appearance in the commercial for Remington also helped to raise her profile, solidifying her place as one of the most successful and influential female singers of all time.

Linda Ronstadt's second solo album, Silk Purse, was released in March of 1970. Recorded entirely in Nashville and produced by Elliot Mazer, the album featured a collection of country, rock, and folk songs. The album was a natural progression from her debut album and showcased her growing talent as a singer and songwriter.

The album begins with the single "Lover's Return," a classic country ballad about a woman who is longing for her lover to come home. Ronstadt's voice is soft yet powerful, and her guitar playing gives the track an added layer of emotion. Other highlights on the album include the country-rocker "Long Long Time," the jazzy "Willin'," and the hauntingly beautiful "You're No Good."

The majority of the songs on Silk Purse were written or co-written by Ronstadt, showcasing her ever-evolving songwriting style. The lyrics often draw on personal experience and emotion, as Ronstadt reflects on love, heartbreak, and the pain of growing up. Her voice is equally as impressive, as she expertly navigates her way through each track, delivering a raw and powerful vocal performance.

The album also showcases Ronstadt's impressive range as a vocalist. From the upbeat, country-tinged "Long Long Time" to the soulful ballad "I Ain't Always Been Faithful" to the tender folk tune "Silver

Threads and Golden Needles," Ronstadt showcases her versatility as a singer.

Silk Purse is a stunning showcase of Ronstadt's talents as a singer and songwriter. She takes the listener on a journey through a range of emotions and styles, and her impressive vocal performance is sure to leave listeners in awe. From the opening track to the closing notes of "Willin'," Ronstadt delivers a powerful and captivating performance that is sure to please both country and pop fans alike.

Ronstadt has stated that she was not pleased with the album, claiming that it was "too lightweight". The album was well-received by critics, however, and provided Ronstadt with her first solo hit in the form of the multi-format single "Long, Long Time". It also earned her a Grammy nomination for Best Contemporary Vocal Performance/Female. The album was a departure from the folk-rock sound of her debut album and instead featured a more country-influenced sound.

The album included cover versions of songs by Hank Williams, Johnny Cash, and Patsy Cline, as well as original songs written by Ronstadt and her then-manager Peter Asher. The album also featured a duet with Glen Campbell on the track "Falling in Love Again". Despite its commercial success, Silk Purse was not as well-received by Ronstadt as her debut album. Ronstadt has stated that she felt the album was too lightweight and not as musically ambitious as her debut. She has also expressed dissatisfaction with her vocal performances on the album, claiming that her voice was still too immature. Ronstadt's third solo album, Linda Ronstadt, was released in 1971 and was a marked departure from the country-influenced sound of Silk Purse. This album featured a more rock-based sound and was more in line with the sound of her debut album. The album was a commercial and critical success and helped to establish Ronstadt as one of the most popular female singers of the 1970s.

Chapter 5:

Touring

Linda Ronstadt is an iconic singer-songwriter who has been delighting fans since the late 1960s. She has had an incredible career that has seen her perform with some of the most famous and talented musicians of her time, including Jackson Browne, the Eagles, Toots, and the Maytals.

Ronstadt began her career as a folk singer in the late 1960s before transitioning to a more country-rock sound. She was one of the first female artists to gain recognition in the male-dominated music industry and established herself as a formidable vocalist and songwriter.

In the early 1970s, Ronstadt began performing with Jackson Browne, who had been a longtime friend. The two collaborated on several songs, including "You're No Good," which became a hit single. The two toured together throughout the 1970s, performing a blend of folk and country rock.

In 1974, Ronstadt joined the Eagles and became a permanent member of the band. She contributed her powerful vocals to the group's hits, such as "Take it Easy" and "Tequila Sunrise," and went on to record three solo albums with the group.

In 1976, Ronstadt performed with the legendary reggae group Toots and the Maytals. The two acts performed a series of shows together, blending reggae, soul, and rock. Ronstadt also recorded a version of

"Monkey Man" with the group, which was released as a single.

Throughout her career, Ronstadt has proven to be an incredibly versatile artist. Her collaborations with Jackson Browne, the Eagles, Toots, and the Maytals show her willingness to explore different genres and styles, and her ability to make all of them sound amazing.

Ronstadt's performances with all three acts have become legendary. Her powerful voice and passionate performances have made her a fan favorite, and her influence on the music industry is undeniable. Fans of all genres can appreciate the amazing music she has made with Jackson Browne, the Eagles, Toots, and the Maytals.

Chapter 6:

Relationships

Linda Ronstadt's relationships with men on a professional level have been complex, tumultuous, and often fraught with issues. In the early days of her career, when she was still an up-and-coming artist, she encountered a lot of competition from her male contemporaries, which often made her feel insecure about her abilities as a musician. This insecurity sometimes led to bad romances and a series of boyfriend managers.

Ronstadt has always been a fiercely independent woman, and this independence often caused tension in her relationships with men. She was not afraid to speak her mind and refused to be controlled by anyone. When she encountered male musicians who tried to take control of her career, she was not afraid to stand her ground and fight for her autonomy. This could lead to strained relationships, which is why she often chose to work with women whenever possible.

Ronstadt was also not afraid to demand respect from her male peers. She was known to put them in their place if they tried to take advantage of her, or if they tried to belittle her accomplishments. This was an attitude that she had to adopt to succeed in an industry dominated by men.

Ronstadt also tended to fall into bad romances with some of the men she encountered in the music industry. She was often drawn to powerful, domineering men, and this often led to unhealthy relationships. These relationships could be draining and destructive, and Ronstadt eventually learned to be more cautious in her romantic life.

Ronstadt eventually learned to be warier than men in her professional life, and she was determined to stand her ground and fight for her autonomy. She was not afraid to speak her mind, and she refused to be controlled by anyone. This enabled her to maintain successful relationships with her male peers, while still asserting her independence.

John Boylan

Linda Ronstadt had a long history in the music industry, and she was no stranger to relationships. In the late 1970s, she began dating John Boylan, an American music producer. He had worked with many of the biggest names in music, including Linda Ronstadt, Joan Baez, and the Eagles.

Ronstadt and Boylan's relationship began in 1979 when Boylan was hired to produce Ronstadt's album Living in the USA. The two had an instant connection, and soon after the album was released, they began dating. In an interview with People Magazine, Ronstadt said about Boylan, "I was smitten. He was everything I was looking for in a man."

The couple was together for three years, and during that time, Ronstadt released two of her most successful albums, Mad Love and Get Closer. Both albums featured production work from Boylan, and the pair had a hand in creating some of Ronstadt's most popular songs, including "Hurts So Bad" and "It's So Easy."

During their time together, the couple traveled extensively, both in the U.S. and abroad. They attended shows and concerts together, and Ronstadt even wrote a song about their time together, "I'm So Lonesome I Could Cry." The couple also made several television appearances together, including The Tonight Show with Johnny Carson and The Merv Griffin Show.

Unfortunately, the couple's relationship eventually came to an end, and Ronstadt moved on to other relationships. She has since spoken fondly of her time with Boylan, saying that "he taught me a lot about music, and he was a great teacher."

While their relationship may have ended, the impact of their time together is still felt today. Not only did Boylan help to create some of Ronstadt's most successful albums, but he also helped to shape her as an artist. He encouraged her to take risks and explore new sounds, and his influence can still be heard in her music today.

Linda Ronstadt and John Boylan's relationship may have been brief, but it was an important part of both of their lives. Though the couple has since parted ways, their time together left a lasting mark on the music industry and the hearts of fans everywhere.

Peter Asher

Linda Ronstadt and Peter Asher were one of the most iconic couples of the late 1960s and early 1970s. The two met in 1966 when Linda was just 18 and Peter was 21. Linda auditioned for The Stone Poneys, a folk-rock band that Peter was a part of, and the two instantly connected. They began dating shortly after, and a few months later, they moved into a house in Laurel Canyon.

The couple quickly became a fixture in the Los Angeles music scene. They supported each other in their musical endeavors and attended numerous music events together. Peter was Linda's musical mentor, and he helped her find her signature sound. Linda learned a lot from Peter and credited him with helping her become the artist she was.

The couple stayed together for three years, during which time they worked together on Linda's first three solo albums. Peter acted as Linda's producer, and he was instrumental in helping her find her style within the music industry. Peter had a huge influence on Linda's music, and he is often credited with helping her find her signature sound.

The couple also worked together in their private lives. They attended parties and events together, and Linda often took Peter's advice in matters of music and beyond. Linda and Peter were deeply in love, and they shared a strong bond.

Sadly, the relationship ended in 1969. Linda wanted to focus on her career, and Peter wanted to move into music management. They parted on good terms and remained friends for the rest of their lives.

Even though the relationship ended, Linda and Peter's time together was extremely special. They shared a deep connection and had a great influence on each other's lives and careers. Linda and Peter's relationship was an important part of the history of music, and it will continue to be remembered for years to come.

J.D. Souther

It was in the early 1970s when Linda Ronstadt and J.D. Souther first met at a music festival in California. The two quickly developed a strong bond and romantic relationship, which would last for several years.

At the start of their relationship, Linda and J.D. were both heavily involved in the music scene. Linda was a successful and respected singer, songwriter, and producer, while J.D. was a talented songwriter and musician. Together, they created some of the most iconic songs of the decade, including "You're No Good," "Silver Threads and Golden Needles," and "Faithless Love."

Although their relationship was centered on music, their bond was deeper than that. Being around each other seemed to bring out the best in each of them. Linda described their relationship as "magical," and J.D. could not help but feel inspired by Linda's passion and talent.

Throughout their time together, Linda and J.D. shared many memories and experiences that would last a lifetime. From romantic dates in California to intimate studio sessions in Nashville, the two were always having fun and creating music.

Unfortunately, after more than two years of dating, the couple decided to part ways in 1975. While the two remained friends and professional collaborators, they both went on to pursue separate paths.

Despite their split, Linda and J.D.'s relationship had a lasting impact on the music industry. Their unique blend of country, rock, and soul is still heard today, and their songs continue to inspire generations of musicians.

Albert Brooks

The relationship between Linda Ronstadt and Albert Brooks began in 1981 when the two met on the set of the film Modern Romance. Linda Ronstadt had just released her hit album, What's New, while Albert Brooks had just released his first feature film, Real Life. They hit it off immediately and began dating shortly afterward.

Their relationship was highly publicized and the two were often seen out and about together. They attended major events such as the Academy Awards and the Golden Globe Awards and were often seen in the company of other celebrities. Linda Ronstadt and Albert Brooks were an iconic couple and their relationship was highly regarded.

The couple soon became engaged and it seemed as though they were headed for marriage. However, the relationship ended abruptly in 1983 and the two went their separate ways.

Despite their split, the two remained close friends and even collaborated on a few projects. In 1986, Linda Ronstadt and Albert Brooks co-starred in the film Lost in America, and in 1988 they collaborated on the song "You're No Good", which was featured on Linda Ronstadt's album Canciones de mi Padre.

While the romance between Linda Ronstadt and Albert Brooks may have been short-lived, it was a highly publicized and well-regarded one. The two are still friends to this day, and their relationship is remembered as one of the most iconic couples in entertainment.

John Brown

Linda Ronstadt and Jerry Brown's relationship began in the early '80s when the two met in Los Angeles. It was the beginning of a romance that would last for nearly a decade.

The two quickly became very close and Ronstadt even went so far as to write a song about the relationship, "The Governor and Linda". This song was a testament to Ronstadt's admiration for Brown and their bond.

In 1983, Jerry Brown was elected Governor of California and Ronstadt quickly became a vocal supporter of his policies. She was even known to attend political events and rallies with Brown.

The two were often seen together in public, including at the 1984 Democratic National Convention. This only added to the speculation that the two were romantically involved.

The relationship continued for the five years that Brown was Governor, and Ronstadt was often seen attending official state functions with him.

In 1988, the relationship ended abruptly when Brown announced his candidacy for the Democratic Presidential nomination. Ronstadt immediately withdrew her support for Brown and the two went their separate ways.

Ronstadt and Brown never spoke publicly about their relationship, but it's clear that the two had an incredibly close bond. The two had a unique relationship that lasted from 1983 to 1988 and was an important part of Ronstadt's life at the time.

George Lucas

Ronstadt was also in a relationship with Star Wars director George Lucas. The couple became engaged in 1985 Linda Ronstadt and George Lucas have been one of the most talked about couples in Hollywood in recent years. Both have achieved incredible success in their respective fields, so it's no surprise that they have found each other.

Ronstadt was drawn to Lucas's passion for film and storytelling and Lucas was charmed by Ronstadt's music and singing. From there, the two began spending more and more time together. They would go out for dinner, take walks in the park, and attend events together.

Ronstadt was particularly fond of Lucas's creativity and she was extremely impressed by the way he could bring his stories to life on the big screen. The couple's relationship continued to blossom and they even made a joint appearance at the Academy Awards in 2020.

They also took a romantic vacation to Hawaii and were spotted spending quality time together at Lucas's ranch in California. It was clear that the two had a strong connection and that they were truly in love.

They were always seen as a very happy couple and Ronstadt even said that she felt like Lucas was her "soulmate but their engagement was eventually called off in 1988. Ronstadt has since commented on the relationship, stating that the two had different interests and that it wasn't a good match. It was reported that the two had grown apart and were no longer compatible.

Despite the split, they remain on good terms and still keep in touch. Ronstadt and Lucas's relationship was a beautiful and inspiring one. They both achieved tremendous success in their respective fields and it's clear that their relationship had a positive effect on both of them. They may no longer be a couple, but their time together will always be remembered.

Aaron Neville

Linda Ronstadt and Aaron Neville have been dating since 2019, and their relationship has been going strong ever since. The two have become one of the most iconic couples in the music industry, and have been taking their love to the stage with performances of duets.

The couple's first performance together was at the 2019 Grammy Awards, where they sang "I Can't Help Falling in Love". This performance was met with a standing ovation and left the audience mesmerized. It also marked the first time the two had been seen together in public.

Since their first performance, the couple has gone on to perform together multiple times, at various music festivals and special events. Their performances always leave audiences spellbound, as they showcase the power of their love and the strength of their bond.

The two have also collaborated musically, with Ronstadt featuring on several of Neville's albums. They've also written and recorded three songs together, which were released in 2020. These songs, "Peaceful Easy Feeling", "Walking in Memphis", and "Don't Know Much", were all written by the couple, and showcased their beautiful chemistry.

Linda Ronstadt and Aaron Neville are a truly inspirational couple, and their relationship is an example of what true love and commitment can look like. From their public performances to their private moments, they have shown the world that love can conquer all.

The couple has also been quite active in philanthropy and social activism. They have both been involved in numerous charities and organizations, and have used their platform to raise awareness about important issues such as poverty, education, and climate change.

The couple's strong bond and commitment to one another have been an inspiration to many, and their relationship serves as a reminder of the power of love. From their public performances to their private moments, Linda Ronstadt and Aaron Neville have been an example of true love and commitment, and their relationship will continue to be celebrated for years to come.

Jim Carrey

In 1983, Linda Ronstadt and comedian Jim Carrey began a short-lived but highly publicized romance. At the time, Ronstadt was a highly successful singer and Carrey was just beginning his career in stand-up comedy. Their relationship lasted for eight months and was heavily covered by the media. They met through mutual friends and instantly hit it off. Linda is a legendary singer and Grammy Award-winning artist and Jim is an acclaimed comedian and actor. This couple has a lot in common and it's clear to see why they have been head over heels for each other.

The pair have been spending a lot of time together, going on romantic dates and getting to know each other better. From fancy dinners to fun days out, Linda and Jim have been making the most of their relationship. They have also been spotted out and about, enjoying the city and each other's company.

Jim has been supporting Linda in her music career, attending her concerts, and cheering her on. He has also been her rock to lean on during difficult times. They are both incredibly supportive of each other and it is obvious that they have a deep connection.

The couple has been spotted on vacation together, taking in the sights and exploring new places. They have also been attending red-carpet events, showing off their chemistry, and taking plenty of selfies.

It's not just the two of them though, Linda and Jim have also been spending time with their families and friends. They have been making sure that their loved ones get to know each other and have even started planning double dates with their close friends.

Linda and Jim are truly in love and it is evident from their interactions. They have been spotted holding hands, stealing kisses, and just generally enjoying each other's company.

Chapter 7:

Political Views

Ronstadt's politics received both criticism and praise during and after her July 17, 2004, performance at the Aladdin Theatre for the Performing Arts in Las Vegas. During her performance, Ronstadt sang the traditional Mexican song "Desperado" and dedicated it to Michael Moore, the controversial documentary filmmaker who made Bowling for Columbine, Fahrenheit 9/11, and Sicko. This dedication was seen by some as a political statement and led to a chorus of boos from the audience.

According to some reports, Ronstadt was also booed for her comments about the Iraq War and then-President George W. Bush. She asked the audience to "remember why we're in Iraq" and stated her belief that the war was based on lies. This statement was not well-received by some in the crowd.

At the same time, Ronstadt's comments were lauded by those who agreed with her views. Some in the audience cheered her comments and her dedication of the song to Michael Moore. Others applauded her bravery in speaking out against the war.

Following the performance, Ronstadt received both criticism and praise for her outspokenness. Some people accused her of using her platform to espouse her political views and said she should have stuck to singing. Others praised her for her courage and for using her fame to speak out against what she saw as an unjust war.

In the days and weeks that followed, Ronstadt's comments and performance became a major topic of discussion. Some media outlets accused her of using her fame to push a political agenda and dismissed her comments as simply grandstanding. Others praised her for her bravery and for standing up for what she believed in.

Ronstadt's performance and comments have since become a part of her legacy. To some, it stands as an example of the power of celebrity and the ability of one person to make their voice heard. To others, it reinforces the idea that entertainers should stick to entertaining and leave political matters to the politicians. No matter what one's opinion is, it is clear that Ronstadt's performance was a major turning point in her career and an example of how a single person can make a difference.

At a 2006 concert in Canada, Linda Ronstadt made an impassioned statement regarding the current President of the United States, George Bush. She let the Calgary Sun know that she was "embarrassed" that Bush was from the United States, and went on to say that he was an "idiot" and "enormously incompetent on both the domestic and international scenes".

Ronstadt's statement was made with a deep sense of disappointment, as many people throughout the world feel similarly. Bush's unpopularity has been a recurring theme throughout his two terms in office, both in the United States and abroad. His lack of action on foreign policy, particularly with regard to Iraq and Afghanistan, has been a major source of contention, both from his critics and from his party.

Domestically, President Bush has been criticized for his handling of the economy, which has resulted in a major downturn in the US economy. His tax cuts for the wealthy have been seen by many as a move that has done nothing to help the average person and has instead furthered the divide between the rich and the poor.

The Bush administration has also been criticized for its attempts to curtail civil liberties and its lack of transparency. The Patriot Act and other measures have been seen as an infringement on the rights of American citizens, while the administration's overall lack of disclosure has been seen as a move to cover up their actions.

It's no wonder, then, that Linda Ronstadt felt embarrassed by the current President of the United States. As the world watches the Bush administration's actions, it's clear that it has failed to bring the United States closer to its ideals of freedom, justice, and progress.

At home and abroad, President Bush has failed to bring about the change that he promised. His policies have done little to help the US economy, and his foreign policy has been mired in controversy. His lack of transparency and attempts to curtail civil liberties have only served to further alienate him from the public.

It's no surprise, then, that Linda Ronstadt was embarrassed by the current President of the United States. Her statement reflects the feelings of many throughout the world and serves as a reminder of the mistakes the Bush administration has made. As the world awaits the end of the Bush era, it's clear that his legacy will be one of failure and embarrassment.

Ronstadt believes that homophobia is an affront to family values. She believes that, by denying same-sex couples the right to marry, society is sending a message that their relationships are not as valid or important as heterosexual ones. In her view, this is wrong and goes against fundamental principles of family values.

Ronstadt believes that everyone should have the right to marry the person they love, regardless of sexual orientation. She is also a strong advocate for other rights for the LGBT+ community. She feels that society must recognize the importance of love and commitment, no matter who it is between.

Ronstadt has also expressed her support for the LGBT+ community in other ways, such as through her music. She has been known to perform songs with pro-LGBT+ themes, such as "My Blue Heaven", which was written by Irving Berlin and contains lyrics that celebrate same-sex relationships.

Ronstadt is passionate about her mission to ensure that all members of the LGBT+ community are treated with the respect and dignity they deserve. She believes that, by standing up for what is right and fighting for equal rights, we can make a difference in the lives of LGBT+ people everywhere.

Ronstadt's commitment to the cause has been further highlighted by her involvement in events such as the 2012 San Francisco Pride Parade. She has also been an active supporter of the LGBT+ community in other countries, including Mexico, where she has donated proceeds from concerts to organizations that support the LGBT+ community.

Ronstadt believes that it is important to recognize the positive contributions that members of the LGBT+ community have made to society. She has often highlighted the accomplishments of LGBT+ figures in the arts, politics, and business.

Chapter 8:

Achievements

In 2004, Linda Ronstadt wrote the foreword to the book The NPR Curious Listener's Guide to American Folk Music, and in it, she shared her passion for folk music and its importance to American culture. Ronstadt began by noting that folk music has been a part of her life since childhood.

She grew up in a musical family, and her parents had a collection of Mexican and American folk songs that she remembers singing along to. Ronstadt also recalled the days when she would go to the local Mexican market and listen to the traditional music that was played there. She noted that the traditional music she heard was often sad and mournful, but it was also beautiful and full of emotion.

Ronstadt also spoke of how folk music has been used to express the struggles and joys of everyday life. She noted that many of the songs talked about the hardships of life and the struggles of overcoming them. She also highlighted how folk music can be used to celebrate life, with its celebratory songs and dances.

Ronstadt also shared her thoughts on the importance of folk music to America. She noted that folk music is a part of the country's heritage, and it is a reminder of the struggles of the past. She believes that folk music is a way of connecting people to their history and allows them to reflect on their own experiences in life.

Ronstadt further discussed the importance of folk music to the younger generation. She noted that folk music is an important way for young people to express themselves and learn about their history. She highlighted the importance of folk music in teaching the younger generation about the struggles of the past and how to overcome them.

Ronstadt concluded her foreword by noting that folk music has been a part of her life since childhood, and it is something that she will always cherish. She believes that folk music is an important part of American culture, and it is something that should be celebrated and preserved. She is proud to be a part of the folk music community, and she hopes that her words in the foreword will help to inspire others to appreciate the beauty and importance of folk music.

"I am proud to write the foreword to The NPR Curious Listener's Guide to American Folk Music. This book will help listeners explore the dynamic and often overlooked history and diversity of American folk music. From traditional work songs to protest songs, this book will guide curious listeners as they discover the music of the people and explore the cultural and spiritual roots of the genre.

Since I began my career in the 1960s, American folk music has been a major influence in my life. I have been inspired by the music's ability to capture the spirit of the times and the emotion of the human experience. As a performer, I have had a unique vantage point to witness the evolution of the genre and explore its social and political implications.

I have seen firsthand how American folk music has the power to bring people together. From sing-alongs to rallies, this music has provided a platform for people to express themselves and to be heard. Through this book, I hope to encourage listeners to explore and appreciate the richness of American folk music".

Linda Ronstadt has been an integral part of the American music and entertainment industry for more than five decades, and her contributions and influence have been felt across multiple genres of music. She has been honored for her impact on the American arts and was inducted into the Arizona Music & Entertainment Hall of Fame on September 23, 2007.

The Tucson native has had a long, illustrious career in the music business, and her influence has been far-reaching. She was one of the first female artists to have commercial success without having to conform to a particular genre, and she was a major pioneer of the Americana genre. Her catalog spans many genres, including rock, pop, country, folk, Latin, and even opera.

Ronstadt has sold more than 100 million records worldwide, and she has earned 11 Grammy Awards and the Lifetime Achievement Award from the Recording Academy. She has also been inducted into the Rock and Roll Hall of Fame, the Arizona Music and Entertainment Hall of Fame, and the National Broadcasting Hall of Fame.

Ronstadt is an icon of the music industry, and her influence and impact can be heard in the music of many of today's artists. She has also been an advocate for social justice and environmental causes. In addition to her musical accomplishments, she has been a leader in the fight for LGBT rights and was one of the first people to come out publicly in support of same-sex marriage.

Ronstadt's induction into the Arizona Music & Entertainment Hall of Fame is a fitting tribute to her lifetime of achievement and her profound influence on the American arts. She is an icon of American music, and her induction is a recognition of her immense contributions to the industry. Her pioneering spirit, her willingness to challenge the status quo, and her commitment to social justice are all qualities that make her worthy of this honor.

In 2008, Linda Ronstadt was appointed artistic director of the San José Mariachi and Mexican Heritage Festival. The festival, which has been held annually since 2002, celebrates the vibrant culture of the Mexican-American community in the Bay Area.

Ronstadt, who is of Mexican-American descent, has been a passionate supporter of the Mariachi and Mexican Heritage Festival since its inception. She has been a major force in promoting the cultural diversity of the San José area, and her involvement in the festival has been a testament to her commitment to Mexican-American cultural preservation.

Ronstadt has been a vocal advocate of Mariachi music and has dedicated much of her career to the preservation and promotion of the genre. She has performed with some of the most renowned Mariachi groups in Mexico and the United States, including Los Lobos, Conjunto Azteca, La Familia, and Grupo Mazatlán. Her extensive discography of both traditional and contemporary Mariachi music has been instrumental in popularizing the genre.

As part of her duties as artistic director of the San José Mariachi and Mexican Heritage Festival, Ronstadt helps to curate the lineup of performers and collaborates with the production team to create a vibrant and entertaining experience for attendees. She has also been instrumental in expanding the reach of the festival, helping to bring in some of the world's most renowned Mariachi artists.

Linda Ronstadt took to the floor of the United States Congress House Appropriations Subcommittee on Interior, Environment & Related Agencies in April 2010 to convince lawmakers to budget $200 million in the 2010 fiscal year for the National Endowment of the Arts (NEA).

Ronstadt's plea to the Subcommittee was that the NEA is an integral part of the American economy and culture and should be given the necessary funding to ensure its continued success. Ronstadt opened her address to the Subcommittee by noting that the NEA has been a vital resource for every part of the country, from rural areas and small towns to inner cities and suburban communities.

She argued that the NEA has been an invaluable asset to the nation's economy, citing the hundreds of thousands of jobs that it creates and the billions of dollars it generates in economic activity across the United States. Ronstadt went on to point out that the NEA has been a source of inspiration for millions of Americans, from schoolchildren to professional performers.

She argued that the NEA is a key part of the American cultural identity and that its funding is essential for the continued growth of the arts in the United States. She noted that the NEA is an important source of support for artists, providing grants and training to help them reach their creative potential. Ronstadt also highlighted the importance of the NEA's role in preserving American history and culture. She noted that the NEA is a major funder of projects related to American history and that its support is critical to the preservation of our nation's past. She observed that the NEA has been a leader in promoting education and understanding of the arts and that its support is vital to the continued growth of the arts in the United States.

Ronstadt concluded her address to the Subcommittee by noting that the NEA is a major contributor to the nation's economy and culture and deserves the necessary support and funding to ensure its continued success. She argued that the NEA should be given the necessary resources to continue its important work and that the federal government should budget $200 million for the NEA in the 2010 fiscal year.

By allocating the necessary funds to the NEA, Ronstadt argued, the United States would be investing in the future of the arts and helping to ensure the continued growth of the American economy and culture.

In May 2009, Linda Ronstadt was honored with an honorary doctorate of music degree from the Berklee College of Music. The award was given in recognition of Ronstadt's remarkable achievements and influence in music, as well as her contribution to American and international culture.

Ronstadt has earned her place in the pantheon of great American singers. Her career spans five decades, during which time she has released over 30 albums and sold over 50 million records. Her music has bridged the gap between country, rock, folk, and Latin music and made her one of the most successful and influential singers of all time.

Ronstadt's music has resonated with people from all walks of life. From her early hits with the Stone Poneys in the 60s to her later solo recordings, Ronstadt has consistently pushed the boundaries of music. Her willingness to explore new sounds and bring together different genres has earned her a legion of fans.

Ronstadt has also been an advocate for the rights of women and minorities in the music industry. She has used her fame and influence to support those who have been marginalized and excluded from the mainstream. She was instrumental in creating a platform for female singer-songwriters to gain recognition and appreciation.

Ronstadt's music has been embraced by fans around the world. She has performed sold-out concerts in the United States, Europe, and Latin America. Her songs have been covered by other artists, and she has been recognized with numerous awards, including the Grammy Lifetime Achievement Award and the National Medal of Arts.

The Berklee College of Music's recognition of Ronstadt's contribution to music and culture is a testament to her lasting influence. The honor is a reminder to aspiring musicians of the power of music to bring people together. Ronstadt's music has inspired generations of musicians, and her legacy will continue to touch the hearts of many for years to come.

Linda Ronstadt has won 11 Grammy Awards, making her one of the most decorated female artists in the history of the awards. She was first honored with a Grammy Award in 1975, when she won Best Country Vocal Performance for her hit single "When Will I Be Loved". She went on to win her first Album of the Year award in 1976 for her album "Hasten Down the

Wind". In 1979, she became the first female artist to win a Record of the Year award for her hit single "Ooh Baby Baby".

Ronstadt won her second Album of the Year award in 1983 for her album "What's New". She won two more awards in 1985 for Best Female Pop Vocal Performance for her single "You're No Good" and Best Pop Vocal Performance by a Duo or Group for her collaboration with Dolly Parton on "Trio".

In 1988, Ronstadt won Best Pop Vocal Performance by a Female for her single "Get Closer". She won her last Grammy Award in 1990 for Best Mexican-American Performance for her album "Canciones de Mi Padre".

Linda Ronstadt is an iconic singer and songwriter who has achieved immense success over the course of her career. She has sold more than 100 million albums, making her one of the most successful female artists of all time. Ronstadt has also had 38 singles on the Billboard Hot 100 charts, a testament to her lasting popularity.

Ronstadt first broke into the charts in 1969 with her cover of Buddy Holly's "It's So Easy", and she quickly rose to the top of the charts with her next single, "Long, Long Time". This song reached the number five spot, and it set the stage for Ronstadt's long career in pop music.

In the 1970s, Ronstadt had a string of successful singles, including "You're No Good" and "When Will I Be Loved". Both of these songs reached the top 10 of the Billboard Hot 100 charts, and they remain fan favorites to this day. She also had several other singles that reached the top 40, such as "Heat Wave" and "Desperado".

Ronstadt's success continued in the 1980s, when she had a series of top 10 hits, including "Blue Bayou", "What's New", and "How Do I Make You". She also had several other singles that reached the top 40, such as "You're Only Lonely", "Get Closer", and "Somewhere Out There".

Ronstadt's success continued into the 1990s, when she had a string of top 40 hits, including "Heartache Tonight", "Don't Know Much", "When Something Is Wrong With My Baby", and "Winter Light". She also had several other singles that reached the top 40, such as "Feels Like Home", "Adios", and "I Can't Let Go".

In the 2000s, Ronstadt had several singles that reached the top 40, such as "Lovin', Touchin', Squeezin'", "Crazy Love", and "I Can't Stop Loving You". She also had several other singles that reached the top 40, such as "Tracks of My Tears", "Adios", and "I Can't Let Go".

Ronstadt's 38 singles on the Billboard Hot 100 charts are a testament to her lasting popularity and success. Her ability to adapt to different genres and create timeless hits has made her one of the most successful female artists of all time. In addition to her singles, she has also released several successful albums, including Heart Like a Wheel, Simple Dreams, and Living in the USA, all of which have sold millions of copies. Ronstadt's music continues to be enjoyed by many, and her singles on the Billboard Hot 100 charts serve as a reminder of her lasting legacy.

Chapter 9:

Conclusion

Linda Ronstadt is an iconic singer, songwriter, musician, producer, and actress whose career has spanned over five decades. Her music has inspired countless others to pursue their dreams and has earned her numerous awards including multiple Grammy Awards, an Emmy, and a Lifetime Achievement Award. She has also been inducted into the Rock and Roll Hall of Fame and the Songwriters Hall of Fame. Linda Ronstadt's music has been a major influence in the popular music industry, and she has been an inspiration for many current musical artists. Her career has been an example of how to combine musical genius with professionalism and dedication to her craft.

Linda Ronstadt has been a major influence in the music industry, not only with her iconic music but also with her unwavering commitment to her craft and her positive influence on the music industry. She has produced many timeless albums, collaborated with a range of incredible artists, and produced some truly amazing music. Linda Ronstadt has used her talents for good to help promote social issues and to bring joy to her fans around the world. Her music will continue to inspire and be heard for many years to come.

Linda Ronstadt is an incredible artist and a true icon of the music industry. She has influenced countless other artists to follow their dreams and has produced some of the most iconic music of all time. Her career has been an example of the power of music and how it can bring joy and inspiration to the world. Her commitment to her art and her passion for her craft will continue to be an inspiration to generations to come. Linda Ronstadt will always be remembered as one of the greatest singers, songwriters, and musicians of all time.